NATURE'S CHILDREN

MANATEES

by Katie Marsico

Children's Press®

An Imprint of Scholastic Inc.

New York Toronto London Auckland Sydney
Mexico City New Delhi Hong Kong
Danbury, Connecticut

Content Consultant
Dr. Stephen S. Ditchkoff
Professor of Wildlife Sciences
Auburn University
Auburn, Alabama

Photographs © 2013: age fotostock: 31 (Andre Seale), 8 (H.
Schmidbauer), 35 (Universal Images Group); Bob Italiano: 44
foreground, 45 foreground; Dreamstime/Jandiver: 2 background,
3 background, 44 background, 45 background; Getty Images: 39
(Ben Horton/National Geographic), 24 (Brian J. Skerry/National
Geographic), 12 (Carol Grant); Media Bakery: cover (T. O'Keefe/
PhotoLink), 5 bottom, 19 (Tom Brakefield); National Geographic
Stock/Mauricio Handler: 20; Photo Researchers: 28 (Chris Hellier),
23 (Clay Coleman), 40 (Douglas Faulkner), 36 (Jeffrey Greenberg);
Shutterstock, Inc./Liquid Productions, LLC: 27; Superstock, Inc.: 7
(age fotostock), 32 (Minden Pictures), 1, 2 foreground, 3
foreground, 15, 46 (NaturePL), 4, 5 background, 16 (NHPA),
5, 11 (Wayne Lynch/All Canada Photos).

Library of Congress Cataloging-in-Publication Data
Marsico, Katie, 1980–
   Manatees/by Katie Marsico.
      p. cm.—(Nature's children)
   Includes bibliographical references and index.
   ISBN-13: 978-0-531-26835-3 (lib. bdg.)
   ISBN-13: 978-0-531-25480-6 (pbk.)
   1. Manatees—Juvenile literature. I. Title.
QL737.S63M3627 2013
599.55—dc23   2012000646

All rights reserved. Published in 2013 by Children's Press, an imprint
of Scholastic Inc.
Printed in China 62
SCHOLASTIC, CHILDREN'S PRESS, and associated logos are
trademarks and/or registered trademarks of Scholastic Inc.

1 2 3 4 5 6 7 8 9 10 R 22 21 20 19 18 17 16 15 14 13

Manatees

Class	Mammalia
Order	Sirenia
Family	Trichechidae
Genus	*Trichechus*
Species	*Trichechus inunguis* (Amazonian manatees), *Trichechus senegalensis* (West African manatees), *Trichechus manatus* (West Indian manatees)
World distribution	The waters of the southeastern United States, the Caribbean, Central America, South America, and West Africa
Habitats	Primarily slow-moving rivers, bays, and estuaries
Distinctive physical characteristics	Gray or grayish-brown, oval-shaped body that is covered with sparse, thin hairs; paddle-shaped tail; small eyes; snout with whiskers
Habits	Migratory; neither completely social nor solitary; generally slow moving, but can travel faster in short bursts; sleeps for several short periods during both day and night; surfaces to breathe air every few minutes
Diet	Mainly feeds on sea grasses and other aquatic plants; can eat up to 10 percent of its body weight on a daily basis

MANATEES

Contents

CHAPTER 1

6 Spectacular Sea Cows

CHAPTER 2

10 Surviving in a Watery World

CHAPTER 3

21 A Look at a Manatee's Life

CHAPTER 4

29 Manatees Past and Present

CHAPTER 5

37 In Danger of Dying Out

42 Words to Know

44 Habitat Map

46 Find Out More

47 Index

48 About the Author

Spectacular Sea Cows

At first, the surface of a slow-moving Florida river appears calm and still. Yet every few minutes, a whiskered snout pokes above the water. The large, gray nostrils are part of the wrinkled face of an aquatic animal called a manatee.

These creatures are also known as sea cows. People who have seen a manatee up close usually understand why this nickname fits. Manatees slowly move their bulky, oval-shaped bodies through shallow water as they search for their next meal. Like actual cows, manatees are herbivores. This means they feed only on plants.

Manatees often weigh more than 1,000 pounds (454 kilograms), but they are far from ferocious. Manatees are gentle giants. Scientists do not believe that they have any natural enemies in the wild.

Manatees must raise their noses above the water's surface to breathe.

Speed and Size

Manatees do far more than bob up and down in the water. They usually swim between 3 and 5 miles per hour (5 and 8 kilometers per hour) but have been known to reach speeds of 20 mph (32 kph).

Adult manatees are about 10 feet (3 meters) long and usually weigh between 800 and 1,200 pounds (363 and 544 kg). Their large bodies have led some people to say that they look like giant gray rocks.

Manatees have thinner layers of body fat than other aquatic mammals such as whales. As a result, they are easily affected by the cold and tend to avoid waters cooler than 70 degrees Fahrenheit (21 degrees Celsius). Cold water causes manatees to eat less, lose weight, and get sick. Some even die from a condition that scientists call cold stress.

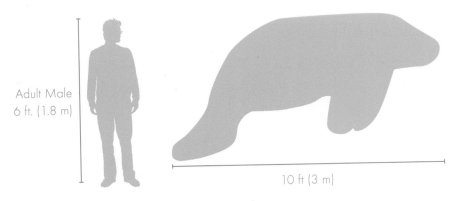

Adult Male
6 ft. (1.8 m)

10 ft (3 m)

Manatees are large but graceful aquatic animals.

CHAPTER 2

Surviving in a Watery World

Scientists believe that manatees have existed on Earth for tens of millions of years. What exactly has allowed manatees to survive for so long in their watery world?

It is important to keep in mind that these creatures are mammals, not fish. They must submerge to feed but cannot breathe underwater. Manatees must raise their nostrils above the surface of the water to breathe air just as humans and other land animals do. Special valves in a manatee's nostrils close when it submerges. This stops water from flowing through its nose and into its lungs.

Manatees usually surface to breathe about every three to four minutes. In some cases, they can remain underwater for much longer. Manatees have been known to stay submerged for up to 20 minutes at a time.

Manatees can hold their breath for a long time.

Powerful Lungs and Buoyant Bodies

One reason manatees are able to remain underwater so long is that they take in much more oxygen with each breath than humans do. Manatees replace 90 percent of the oxygen in their lungs with every breath. This is nine times more air than average human beings renew when they breathe in! Because manatees get so much oxygen with each breath, they do not need to breathe as often. This incredible respiratory system also allows the manatee to control its buoyancy, or ability to float, by adjusting the amount of air in its body.

Manatees are extremely buoyant. Luckily they have special physical traits that stop them from simply floating away. Scientists believe that many of their bones do not contain marrow. This makes their bones much heavier and weighs them down in the water. Having no marrow in their bones also allows manatees to move straight up and down when they surface and submerge.

Manatees can float upward quickly when they need to breathe.

Made for Aquatic Movement

Manatees are often on the move—whether in search of warm water or the aquatic plant life that makes up their diet. These mammals may be big, but they are skilled swimmers.

Manatees use two pectoral flippers on the upper part of their body to steer through the water and to move food toward their mouth. They do not have any hind flippers. They do, however, have powerful tails that look similar to paddles. Manatees swim by moving their bodies and tails up and down. Much of a manatee's body is streamlined. This means that its shape allows it to glide gracefully through the water.

Most manatees can swim in both freshwater and saltwater. Their kidneys are excellent at removing salt from their bloodstream. This allows them to swim in saltwater without getting sick.

FUN FACT! Because they do not need to chase their food, manatees are slower than animals such as dolphins.

Manatees use their huge tails to propel themselves through the water.

A Sea Cow's Senses

Manatees rely on their senses while swimming. Their eyes are small but allow them to tell objects apart based on size and color. They can also detect different levels of brightness. This helps them locate aquatic plants in dark or murky waters.

Scientists believe that manatees may have a good sense of hearing as well. Manatees use their ears to hear the chirps, whistles, and squeaks that they use to communicate with each other. Yet it seems unlikely that the animals can hear extremely low-pitched sounds, such as the noise of nearby boat engines.

Scientists are still trying to find out just how strong manatees' senses of taste and smell are. However, they are fairly sure that manatees rely heavily on touch and body contact. Manatees probably even use the whiskers on their snouts and the small hairs on their bodies to sense the world around them!

Manatees' eyes may be small, but they are useful when it comes to locating food underwater.

Tremendous Teeth

Sometimes the plants that manatees eat are tough or coated with sand. It is not surprising that a manatee's eating habits can quickly wear down its teeth.

Fortunately, manatees' mouths are able to handle their diet. Most of a manatee's teeth are molars that can be replaced over and over again once they are worn down. Scientists call them marching molars because of the way they move forward in the mammals' mouths.

Manatees grow marching molars toward the back of their jaws. Over time, these teeth push closer to the front of their mouths. After a while, they become worn down and fall out. Then new molars move forward to replace them. This cycle is repeated countless times throughout a manatee's life.

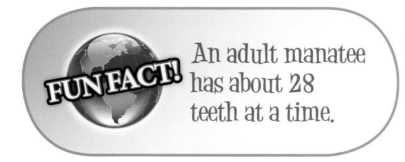

FUN FACT! An adult manatee has about 28 teeth at a time.

Manatees have wide, flat teeth.

CHAPTER 3

A Look at a Manatee's Life

Manatees are found in the waters of the southeastern United States, the Caribbean, Central America, South America, and West Africa. They spend time in slow-moving rivers and shallow bays and estuaries. Estuaries are areas where freshwater and saltwater mix when a river empties into the sea.

Manatees **migrate** throughout the year as seasons change. They move to new areas in search of warmer temperatures. Manatees can cover a large distance within a short period of time. Scientists who tracked one female manatee observed that she traveled 150 miles (241 km) in less than four days!

Most manatees prefer to stay in shallow water. They usually do not swim deeper than 7 feet (2 m) beneath the surface. Sometimes manatees submerge and sleep at the bottom of waterways. They sleep for short periods throughout both daytime and nighttime hours.

Sleeping manatees must wake up every few minutes to breathe.

Hungry Herbivores

Manatees are usually eating whenever they aren't sleeping. Their favorite foods are aquatic plants such as sea grasses. Manatees graze on the sandy bottoms of waterways. They also forage for plants that float or poke above the water's surface.

Manatees can eat up to 10 percent of their body weight every day. This means a single 1,000-pound (454 kg) sea cow might feed on as much as 100 pounds (45 kg) of aquatic plants within 24 hours!

Manatees use their flippers and lips to pull food toward their mouths. A manatee's upper lip is split into two parts. Each part is flexible and can move on its own to grab hold of aquatic plants.

Most manatees search for food in both freshwater and saltwater environments, but they do not drink saltwater. Scientists believe that this is why all manatees must seek out freshwater every one to two weeks.

FUN FACT! Manatees sometimes eat tiny animals by accident while they are grazing on underwater plants.

Manatees eat the plants that sprout up from the bottoms of shallow waterways.

Social or Solitary?

Manatees are neither completely social nor completely solitary. They do not spend much time in groups but are not always by themselves either. Because they face few predators, manatees do not rely on large groups for extra protection in the wild. Yet scientists believe that they still communicate with one another by squeaking, grunting, and chirping.

From time to time, manatees gather together in temporary herds. This is often because they are all seeking out an area with warmer temperatures, food, or freshwater. They also form herds when they are ready to mate.

Female manatees, or cows, are able to have babies when they are between three and five years old. Males, or bulls, begin mating when they are between the ages of three and four years old. Cows usually give birth to a single baby, or calf, every two to five years. The calf is born approximately 12 months after its parents mate.

Manatees sometimes travel in small groups.

Birth and Beyond

Newborn manatee calves measure about 3 to 4 feet (0.9 to 1.2 m) long and weigh about 60 to 70 pounds (27 to 32 kg). Like other mammals, they feed on their mothers' milk. Manatee calves often drink milk until they are about one year old.

Calves sometimes stay with their mothers for as long as two years after birth. The young manatees learn important survival skills as they grow. They begin swimming and communicating soon after they are born. They also start learning to forage for aquatic plants when they are only a few weeks old.

A healthy manatee can survive in the wild for as long as 60 years. Unfortunately many do not live that long. Scientists recently discovered that most of the manatees they studied were dying before the age of 30. This is one of the reasons why conservationists are trying to learn more about the world's sea cows—and how to help them survive.

Calves form close relationships with their mothers.

CHAPTER 4

Manatees Past and Present

Manatee ancestors existed on Earth almost as long ago as dinosaurs did. Scientists believe that the last dinosaurs died out roughly 65 million years ago. The oldest manatee fossils date back about 55 million to 60 million years. Yet they do not show the exact same mammal that people think of when they picture today's sea cows.

Scientists believe that manatees are closely related to elephants, aardvarks, and animals called hyraxes. Hyraxes look similar to large guinea pigs or rabbits. Scientists think that manatees' earliest ancestors were four-footed mammals that lived on land!

These creatures probably waded into the water to search for plants to eat. Scientists suspect that these animals' bodies slowly changed as they spent more time in the water. Each generation was better at swimming than the previous one was. Fossils dating back about 13 million to 16 million years show mammals that look similar to modern manatees.

Fossils have helped scientists learn about manatees' ancestors.

Different Species of Sea Cow

Today, three different species of manatee swim through the world's waters—the West Indian manatee, the Amazonian manatee, and the West African manatee. More West Indian manatees live in the southeastern United States than anywhere else. They are often spotted in Florida or other states that are close to the Atlantic Ocean or the Gulf of Mexico. West Indian manatees also live throughout Mexico, the Caribbean, Central America, and South America.

Amazonian manatees live in South America. These sea cows spend all of their time in a freshwater environment. They are found in the continent's long, winding Amazon River. Amazonian manatees are smaller than the West Indian species.

West African manatees swim along West Africa's Atlantic coast. Like West Indian manatees, they cruise through both freshwater and saltwater environments. Unfortunately, scientists have not been able to do much research on West African or Amazonian manatees. They have mainly studied the West Indian species in Florida.

Amazonian manatees never leave their river habitat.

Sirenian Relatives

Manatees are sometimes confused with animals called dugongs. These two creatures are closely related. Both belong to the same scientific order—Sirenia. All sirenians are plant-eating mammals that live in an aquatic environment. Like manatees, dugongs have flippers toward the front of their bodies but none near the back end. However, there are a few important differences between the two animals that set them apart.

Dugongs' tails are shaped more like fins than broad paddles. In addition, the males sometimes grow tusks. Dugong tusks look similar to the long, pointed teeth that stick out of a walrus's closed mouth.

Finally, manatees tend to live in different parts of the world than their dugong cousins. Dugongs are mainly found in Asia, Africa, and Australia along the Indian and Pacific Oceans. Unlike manatees, they never swim in freshwater. Sadly, scientists believe that dugongs may also become endangered if more is not done to protect them.

Dugongs closely resemble manatees.

The Steller's Sea Cow

The Steller's sea cow provides an example of what could happen to manatees if people do not take action to save them. This aquatic mammal is an extinct sirenian. It used to live in a part of the Pacific Ocean called the Bering Sea. The Bering Sea stretches between Alaska and Siberia and is connected to the Arctic Ocean by the Bering Strait.

The world began to learn more about the Steller's sea cow when a European scientist named Georg Wilhelm Steller began studying it in 1741. According to Steller's research, the mammal was much larger than most average manatees. He reported that it measured 30 feet (9 m) long and weighed roughly 11,500 pounds (5,216 kg) on average!

Scientists did not have much of a chance to learn about the Steller's sea cow in the following years. By the 1760s, hunters had completely killed off these close relatives of manatees.

Georg Wilhelm Steller made several sketches of the aquatic mammal he observed in the 1700s.

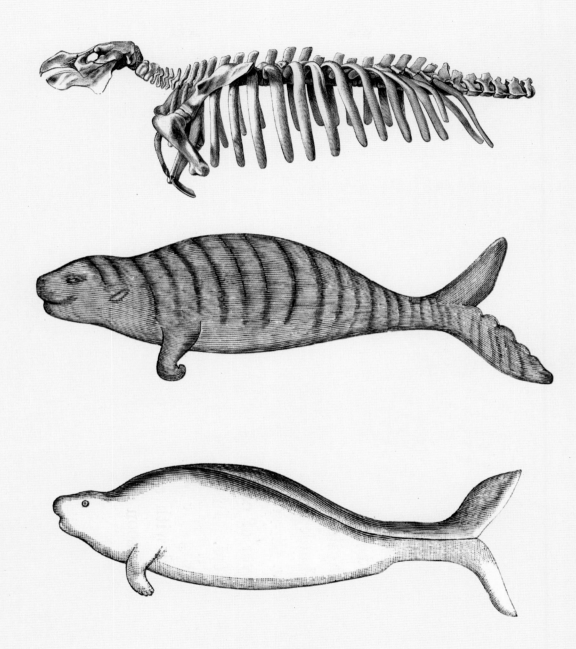

CHAPTER 5

In Danger of Dying Out

Manatees are endangered. This means that scientists are worried they might completely die out. Human beings are the biggest threat to their survival.

Some manatees are killed when boaters accidentally crash into them. In other cases, they become trapped in locks and dams. Fishing equipment is also a threat to manatees. They sometimes get tangled in nets or swallow hooks that fishers cast into the water.

Changes to the environment have also decreased the number of manatees that exist in the wild. Pollution and development along rivers and other coastal areas affect manatees' food supply and living space. Scientists estimate that there are fewer than 5,000 wild manatees left in the United States.

Signs warn boaters to watch out for manatees.

Survival of the Sea Cow

Scientists are doing their best to learn more about manatees. They are working hard with lawmakers and the public to protect these gentle creatures and save them before it is too late. However, sometimes uncontrollable circumstances such as cold weather, diseases, or red tides kill off large numbers of these aquatic mammals. Red tides occur when seawater becomes filled with tiny living things that produce toxins. For the most part, however, human beings have the ability to play a role in the fate of the world's manatees.

Manatees are hunted in certain areas, but this is not the most serious threat they face. Collisions with boats and the loss of their habitat are much bigger problems. Boaters moving at high speeds often do not see manatees in the water until it is too late. Boat propellers and pollution also take a toll on sea grass beds. This destroys the aquatic plant life that manatees rely on to survive.

Boat propellers can leave manatees with serious injuries and lifelong scars.

Efforts to Prevent Extinction

Scientists, government leaders, and the public must all work together to prevent manatees from becoming extinct. People have created laws that are designed to protect sea cows. In many cases, government officials have developed rules that limit the speed of boats in waters where manatees are known to swim.

Others have formed sanctuaries that boaters are not allowed to enter. They hope that setting aside these areas will decrease the number of manatee deaths that result from boat injuries or destruction to sea grass beds.

It is important that human beings understand how their actions affect manatees. Scientists are working hard, but they still have much to learn. The more that people discover about manatees, the clearer it becomes that they must do everything in their power to save these gentle aquatic giants.

Scientists study manatees at sanctuaries so we can learn how to better protect these amazing animals.

Words to Know

ancestors (AN-ses-turz) — ancient animal species that are related to modern species

aquatic (uh-KWAH-tik) — living or growing in water

collisions (kuh-LIH-zhuhnz) — crashes that occur when two objects slam into one another

conservationists (kon-sur-VAY-shun-ists) — people who work to protect an environment and the living things in it

endangered (en-DAYN-jurd) — at risk of becoming extinct, usually because of human activity

environments (en-VYE-ruhn-mints) — surroundings in which an animal lives or spends time

extinct (ik-STINGKT) — no longer found alive

forage (FOR-ij) — search for food

fossils (FOSS-uhlz) — the hardened remains of prehistoric plants and animals

generation (jen-uh-RAY-shun) — animals or individuals born around the same time

graze (GRAZE) — to feed on grasses or other plants

herbivores (HUR-buh-vorz) — animals that only eat plants

herds (HURDZ) — groups of animals that stay together or move together

mammals (MAM-uhlz) — warm-blooded animals that have hair or fur and usually give birth to live young

marrow (MAR-oh) — the soft substance inside bones

mate (MAYT) — to join together to produce babies

migrate (MY-grayt) — to move from one area to another

molars (MOH-lurz) — wide, flat teeth at the back of the mouth used for crushing and chewing food

order (OR-duhr) — a category that groups different families of animals together according to similar traits that they share

pectoral (PEK-tuh-ruhl) — toward an animal's chest or the front of its body

pollution (puh-LOO-shuhn) — harmful materials that damage or contaminate the air, water, and soil

predators (PREH-duh-turz) — animals that live by hunting other animals for food

respiratory system (RES-pur-uh-tor-ee SIS-tuhm) — the group of organs that is responsible for breathing

sanctuaries (SANGK-choo-er-eez) — natural areas where animals are protected from hunters or other dangers

snout (SNOUT) — the long front part of an animal's head, including the nose, mouth, and jaws

species (SPEE-sheez) — one of the groups into which animals and plants of the same genus are divided

submerge (suhb-MURJ) — to sink below the surface of the water

toxins (TAHKS-inz) — poisonous substances

valves (VALVZ) — body structures containing a flap that allows fluids to flow only one way through them

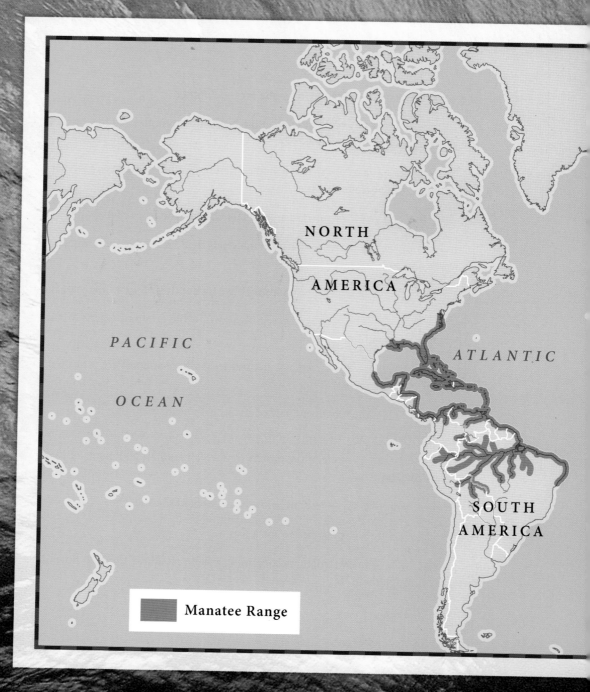

NORTH AMERICA

PACIFIC

OCEAN

ATLANTIC

SOUTH AMERICA

Manatee Range

ARCTIC OCEAN

EUROPE

ASIA

AFRICA

PACIFIC OCEAN

OCEAN

INDIAN

OCEAN

AUSTRALIA

Find Out More

Books

Goldish, Meish. *Florida Manatees: Warm Water Miracles*. New York: Bearport Publishing, 2008.

King, Zelda. *Manatees*. New York: PowerKids Press, 2012.

Lourie, Peter. *The Manatee Scientists: Saving Vulnerable Species*. Boston: Houghton Mifflin Books for Children, 2011.

Otfinoski, Steven. *Manatees*. New York: Marshall Cavendish Benchmark, 2011.

Skerry, Brian. *Face to Face with Manatees*. Washington, D.C.: National Geographic, 2010.

Swinburne, Stephen. *Saving Manatees*. Honesdale, PA: Boyds Mills Press, 2006.

Visit this Scholastic Web site for more information on manatees:
www.factsfornow.scholastic.com
Enter the keyword **Manatees**

Index

Amazonian manatees, 30, *31*

babies. *See* calves.
boats, 17, *36*, 37, 38, *39*, 41
body temperatures, 9, 21, 25
bones, 13
breathing, *7*, 10, *11*, *12*, 13, *20*
bulls, 25
buoyancy, *12*, 13

calves, 25, 26, *27*
color, 6, 9
communication, 17, 25, 26
conservation, 26, 38, *40*, 41
cows, 25, *27*

dugongs, *32*, 33

ears, 17
endangered species, 33, 37
extinction, 34, 41
eyes, *16*, 17

females. *See* cows.
flippers, 14, 22, 33
food. *See* milk; plants.
foraging, 6, 14, 22, 26
fossils, *28*, 29
freshwater, 14, 21, 22, 25, 30, 33

groups. *See* herds.

habitats, 21, 30, *31*, 33, 34, 38
herbivores, 6
herds, *24*, 25
humans, 10, 13, *36*, 37, 38, *40*, 41

length, 9, *9*, 26
life spans, 26

males. *See* bulls.
marching molars, 18
mating, 25
migration, 21
milk, 26

nickname, 6
noses. *See* snouts.

plants, 6, 14, 17, 18, 22, *23*, 25, 26, 29,
    33, 37, 38, 41
pollution, 37, 38
population, 37
predators, 6, 25, 34, 38
prehistoric manatees, *28*, 29

red tides, 38

saltwater, 14, 21, 22, 30
sanctuaries, *40*, 41
senses, 17
Sirenia order, 33, 34
sizes, 6, 8, 9, *9*, 26, 30, 34

(Index continued)

sleeping, *20*, 21
snouts, 6, *7*, 10, 17
species, 30
speeds, 9, 14, 21
Steller, Georg Wilhelm, 34
Steller's sea cows, 34, *35*
swimming, 9, 10, *11*, 13, 14, *15*, 17,
    21, 26, 29, 30, 41

tails, 14, *15*, 33
teeth, 18, *19*, 33

weight, 6, 9, 13, 22, 26, 34
West African manatees, 30
West Indian manatees, 30
whiskers, 6, 17

About the Author

Katie Marsico is the author of more than 100 children's books. She hopes to one day see a manatee in the wild when she visits her favorite place in the world—Florida.